COLOMBIA

By Sloane Gould
and Alicia Z. Klepeis

EXPLORING WORLD CULTURES

Cavendish Square

Published in 2026 by Cavendish Square Publishing, LLC
2544 Clinton Street, Buffalo, NY 14224

Second Edition

Library of Congress Cataloging-in-Publication Data

Names: Klepeis, Alicia, 1971- author. | Gould, Sloane, author.
Title: Colombia / Alicia Z. Klepeis
Description: Second edition / Sloane Gould. | Buffalo, New York : Cavendish Square Publishing, 2026. | Series: Exploring world cultures | Includes index.
Identifiers: LCCN 2024038124 (print) | LCCN 2024038125 (ebook) | ISBN 9781502673459 (library binding) | ISBN 9781502673442 (paperback) | ISBN 9781502673466 (ebook)
Subjects: LCSH: Colombia--Juvenile literature.
Classification: LCC F2258.5 .K55 2025 (print) | LCC F2258.5 (ebook) | DDC 986.1--dc23/eng/20241114
LC record available at https://lccn.loc.gov/2024038124
LC ebook record available at https://lccn.loc.gov/2024038125

Writers: Alicia Z. Klepeis; Sloane Gould (second edition)
Editor: Caitie McAneney
Copyeditor: Shannon Harts
Designer: Deanna Lepovich

The photographs in this book are used by permission and through the courtesy of: Cover Hernando Sorzano/ Shutterstock.com; p. 4 Adilson Sochodolak/Shutterstock.com; p. 5 Peter Hermes Furian/Shutterstock.com; p. 6 oscar garces/Shutterstock.com; p. 7 Peter Gudella/Shutterstock.com; pp. 8, 22 Simon Mayer/Shutterstock.com; p. 9 awapanela_photos/Shutterstock.com; p. 10 koldo_studio/Shutterstock.com; p. 11 Gabriel Leonardo Guerrero/ Shutterstock.com; p. 12 mehdi33300/Shutterstock.com; p. 13 afotostock/Shutterstock.com; p. 14 Allen.G/ Shutterstock.com; p. 15 Lautaro Vidal/Shutterstock.com; p. 16 Lexcard/Shutterstock.com; p. 17 DavidAOtalora/ Shutterstock.com; p. 18 ErikAndroid/Shutterstock.com; p. 19 Artush/Shutterstock.com; p. 20 Anamaria Mejia/ Shutterstock.com; pp. 21, 26 Wilmerfotografia/Shutterstock.com; p. 23 SALMONNEGRO-STOCK/ Shutterstock.com; p. 24 lev radin/Shutterstock.com; p. 25 Alexander Canas Arango/Shutterstock.com; p. 27 tony quinn/Alamy Stock Photo; p. 28 Andres Serna Pulido/Shutterstock.com; p. 29 Luis Echeverri Urrea/ Shutterstock.com.

CPSIA compliance information: Batch #CS26CSQ: For further information contact Cavendish Square Publishing LLC at 1-877-980-4450.

Printed in the United States of America

CONTENTS

INTRODUCTION

Located in the northern part of South America, Colombia is known as the "gateway to South America." It borders Panama, a country in Central America. Colombia has an interesting history that includes rich Native **civilizations**, a takeover by the Spanish, and finally, freedom. While Colombia may be free, its citizens have rarely known peace.

The spectacled bear, also called the Andean bear, enjoys the mountainous forests of Colombia.

Colombia's busy cities include Bogotá, Medellín, and Cartagena. In these cities, people live close together. Other Colombians live on farms, on the coast, or even in the rainforest. The people, animals, and plants of Colombia have changed to suit the different landscapes, from the high mountains to the deserts to the wetlands. Colombia's landscape includes the Andes Mountains, which are home to animals found nowhere else on Earth, including the Andean condor and spectacled bear.

This map shows Colombia in the northwestern part of South America.

The **diversity** of Colombia's landscape is much like the diversity of its people and **traditions**. Read on to explore this lively South American country!

GEOGRAPHY

Colombia is a South American country with many diverse and beautiful landscapes. It covers 439,736 square miles (1,138,910 sq km) in area.

The Amazon River basin covers almost half of Colombia. Located in the south of the country, it's made up of thick rainforests. Colombia's rainforests are home to lots of different animals and plants. Toucans, sloths, and one-of-a-kind animals like the golden poison frog live here.

People enjoy the tropical beaches of the Caribbean region, or area, of Colombia.

The Andes Mountains run through the middle of Colombia. Colombia's coasts have **tropical** beaches in the north and west. Huge grasslands, called llanos, are found in the east. Desert areas are found in the north. Along the coasts and in the eastern plains, Colombia has a tropical **climate**, while the mountain areas are cooler.

FACT!
The tallest mountains of Colombia have tropical glaciers. They are in trouble because of global warming.

Pico Cristóbal Colón in Colombia is around 18,950 feet (5,776 meters) tall.

BORDERS

Five countries border Colombia: Brazil, Ecuador, Panama, Peru, and Venezuela. The Pacific Ocean lies in the west, while the Caribbean Sea lies to the north.

HISTORY

Around 20,000 years ago, people arrived in the area that is now Colombia. About 12,000 years ago, people living in the Magdalena Valley of Colombia formed a civilization called the Chibcha, which grew into the Muisca civilization.

In 1499, the first Europeans arrived from Spain. Colombia was then under Spanish control until the early 1800s. After a war with the Spanish in 1819, Colombia became an independent country. Many groups wanted to control the government. This caused civil wars in Colombia that lasted until 2016.

FACT!

In 1819, Simón Bolivar finally led Colombian forces to defeat the Spanish.

Simón Bolivar was a Venezuelan general who freed many South American nations. His monument stands in Bogotá, Colombia.

That year, President Juan Manuel Santos won the Nobel Peace Prize for helping end this long conflict, or period of fighting, with a peace agreement. Today, there is still armed conflict, especially affecting Afro-Colombian, Native, and rural communities.

These are models of ancient Muisca homes in Colombia.

SPANISH CONQUERORS

Spanish explorers arrived in Colombia looking for gold and gems. The Native people tried to protect their land, but were defeated.

GOVERNMENT

Though it is home to conflict and violence, or harm, Colombia is also home to one of South America's oldest democracies. Democracies are governments that give their citizens a voice through voting. Colombia's government has three parts: legislative, executive, and judicial. The legislative part is called the Congress and its job is to write new laws. Colombia's Congress is made up of two houses, the Senate and the Chamber of Representatives.

The Colombian flag is yellow, blue, and red.

The executive part includes the president and the cabinet ministers. The president runs the government and is the head of state. All Colombian citizens over 18 can vote for president and vice president every four years.

Courts make up the judicial part. They follow the country's constitution, or set of basic laws. Colombia's constitution was adopted in 1991.

FACT!
Colombia's government has 32 departments, which are like U.S. states, and one capital district.

In 2022, Colombians elected Gustavo Petro as the first *progressive* president of Colombia.

COLOMBIA'S CAPITAL

The capital of Colombia is Bogotá, which is right in the middle of the country. Colombia's Congress meets at the National Capitol building in Bogotá.

THE ECONOMY

Colombia **exports** many different products around the world. Colombia trades with countries like the United States, China, Panama, and Mexico. Colombian farmers grow crops like coffee, bananas, and sugarcane. Colombia is one of the world's largest producers of cut flowers. They sell more flowers to the United States than any other country. Miners drill for oil and dig for coal, platinum, and emeralds in the ground.

FACT!

Colombia's money is called the peso.

Cartagena is one of the most-visited cities in Colombia.

Tourism, or people visiting from other countries, is a major industry, or business, in Colombia. This provides many jobs in hotels and eateries. Over 60 percent of Colombian workers have service jobs. Some work in stores, schools, and banks. Others work in restaurants, hospitals, and offices. With its goods and services combined, Colombia has the third-largest **economy** in South America.

These raw coffee beans were grown in Colombia.

COFFEE

Coffee sales are a major part of the Colombian economy. Colombia exports 6 million bags of coffee each year!

THE ENVIRONMENT

Colombia is a place of natural beauty, and it's home to a huge number of animals and plants. In the south, the Amazon River basin hosts a rich rainforest ecosystem. Turtles, snakes, and crocodiles live by the river. Anteaters, jaguars, and monkeys live in the thick forests.

FACT!

Spectacled bears live in the cloud forest of the Andes Mountains.

*Colombia is home to the capybara, the largest **rodent** in the world!*

PROTECTING THE ENVIRONMENT

Colombia used to be covered in rich jungles. To save some natural homes for animals, the government has created more than 60 protected areas.

The Andes Mountains in central Colombia are snowy and rocky. The biggest flying bird in the world, the Andean condor, lives here. Below the mountains, the soil is perfect for growing coffee and other crops.

Forests are being cut down in Colombia for farming and mining. This causes soil to wear away and destroys the homes of the animals that live there. Air pollution is also a problem in Colombia. Climate change is leading to more flooding, landslides, **droughts**, and wild weather.

Andean condors live at the highest parts of the Andes Mountains.

THE PEOPLE TODAY

Colombia is home to more than 52 million people of varied backgrounds. Many different groups call Colombia home. More than 87 percent of Colombians are mestizo and white.

The second-largest group of people in Colombia are Afro-Colombian. They have family roots in both Colombia and Africa because enslaved Africans were brought to Colombia hundreds of years ago by the Spanish. They were treated as property. Afro-Colombians make up about 7 percent of the population.

This Indigenous man lives in the Amazon rainforest of Colombia.

Just over 4 percent of Colombians are Indigenous, or Native. The largest Indigenous group is the Wayuu. These Native people mainly live in the La Guajira desert area. They raise livestock and grow crops. Some smaller Indigenous groups are not in contact with the rest of the world.

FACT!

Mestizo means mixed race, usually with Native and white backgrounds.

Afro-Colombian people have woven together rich traditions from both South America and Africa.

INDIGENOUS PEOPLES

Colombia's main Indigenous populations are the Wayuu, Zenú, Nasa, and Pastos. They've suffered from conflict and **displacement**.

LIFESTYLE

Most people in Colombia live a city lifestyle. Cities like Bogotá and Medellín are crowded. There, some people live in apartments. Others live in houses. In the city, people can take a bus or ride a bike to work.

FACT!

More than 80 percent of Colombians live in a city.

More than 11 million people live in Bogotá.

MINERS AT WORK

Mining is a common job in some rural areas. About 350,000 Colombians work in gold mining.

There are also poor, crowded areas outside the city center. Houses here are often small and run-down. In Colombia's countryside, people commonly work on farms. In mountainous areas, there are coffee farms. In the llanos, ranchers raise cattle and other animals. Some families live in **multigenerational** homes, while other homes are just one or two kids and their parents.

In the past, most Colombian women did not work outside the home. Today, about 51 percent of women work outside the home. The literacy rate for boys and girls is about the same, at around 95 percent. Literacy refers to the ability to read.

This Indigenous Colombian lives a rural lifestyle.

RELIGION

Colombia's history of Spanish control is seen in its strong Catholic roots. Around 73 percent of Colombians are Roman Catholic, which was a religion spread by the Spanish. Catholics celebrate holidays like Christmas and Easter. Protestants also celebrate these holidays and follow their own branch of Christianity. About 14 percent of Colombians are Protestant.

FACT!

Some Colombians practice a blend of Roman Catholicism and traditional beliefs that are native to Africa.

La Ermita Church is a Catholic place of worship in Cali, Colombia.

This mosque in La Guajira, Colombia, has a tall tower called a minaret.

There is no official religion, or belief system, in Colombia. In the past, it was considered wrong to practice religions other than Christianity. The right to practice any religion was added to the Colombian constitution in 1991. Today, the nation's Jews tend to live in cities. Colombian Muslims usually live on the nation's Caribbean coast. Some Indigenous Colombians still take part in traditional spiritual practices.

UNDERGROUND RELIGION

One Catholic church is located in an old salt mine—600 feet (180 m) underground! The Cathedral of Zipaquirá was named the First Wonder of Colombia in 2007.

LANGUAGE

The first languages spoken in Colombia were Indigenous languages. There are more than 60 different Native languages spoken in Colombia today. Many Native groups have their own languages. Nasa, Emberá, and Wayuu are a few examples.

FACT!

Colombia is a Hispanic country. That means Spanish is the main language people speak there.

This market has Spanish labels on its peppers.

The Spanish brought their language to Colombia hundreds of years ago. Today, the most common language in Colombia is Spanish. It is also the only official language in Colombia. Colombian children are taught Spanish and sometimes English at school. Colombians typically use Spanish for business. The government uses Spanish too.

Children of Indigenous descent, or backgrounds, often speak two languages–their Native language and Spanish.

Palenquero is a Spanish-based language that was **influenced** by African languages and Portuguese. This is a kind of creole language, or a language with two or more roots. Many Palenquero speakers live in the village of San Basilio de Palenque.

LANGUAGE FAMILIES

The Native languages in Colombia are grouped into 12 different language families.

ARTS AND FESTIVALS

Colombian art and music have a long history. Many Wayuu people make traditional, brightly-colored woven bags called mochilas. Tourists from around the world visit Bogotá's Gold Museum to see gold necklaces, masks, and models. Colombian music is influenced by African, Spanish, and Native beats and instruments. Cumbia is a special dance that started in Colombia's Caribbean region.

FACT!
The Carnival celebration in Barranquilla is the second-largest in the whole world!

Colombian singer Shakira is known around the world for her music.

This statue was made by famous Colombian artist Fernando Botero.

The Colombian people celebrate many festivals. Some are religious, such as El Día de las Velitas, or the Day of the Little Candles. It is celebrated on December 7. On this day, families light hundreds of small candles along the streets. The candles are meant to guide the spirit of Mary, the mother of Jesus, as she travels to bless their homes. Colombians also celebrate Carnival in Barranquilla, a time of dancing, parades, and music.

FLOWER FESTIVAL

Feria de las Flores, or the Flower Festival, is held every year in Medellín at the start of August. People create artwork using brightly-colored flowers.

FUN AND PLAY

If you enjoy having fun outside, Colombia is a great place to live or visit. Cycling, rock climbing, and white water rafting are just a few ways people have fun in nature in Columbia. Along the country's coastline, people also surf and scuba dive. Located north of Bogotá, Suesca is Colombia's best-known rock-climbing spot. It offers adventurous climbers more than 400 different climbing routes to try!

FACT!
On the Caribbean coast, people can visit coral reefs at Corales del Rosario y San Bernardo nature reserve.

This surfer enjoys the waters of Colombia.

Carlos "El Pibe" Valderrama was a famous soccer player in the 1990s in Colombia.

Many Colombians enjoy sports. Soccer is the most popular sport here. People of all ages enjoy playing soccer. Colombia's national sport is *tejo*. Players throw steel discs (called tejos) toward a ring. This ring contains a small parcel filled with gunpowder. If a tejo lands on the ring, it will explode!

CHILDREN'S GAMES

A traditional Colombian kids' game is trompo. Players compete by doing tricks with spinning tops.

FOOD

Colombia's foods show its environment and history. Native fruits include mango, guava, pineapple, and passion fruit. Along the coasts and other waterways, fish is a common ingredient. Often, it is wrapped in leaves and grilled. Near the Caribbean coast, fish is served with coconut rice.

Many Colombian meals have coconut in them, such as this sweet cocada dessert.

PERFECT PATACONES

Colombians enjoy patacones, or tostones, on the side of their meal. They look like pancakes, but are made out of fried plantains.

Arepas are a popular bread-like snack made from corn flour. They can be prepared many ways—stuffed with cheese, meat, or even an egg. *Sancocho* is a delicious soup. It usually holds corn, potatoes, yucca, cilantro, and chicken. People often enjoy it with rice or a slice of avocado.

Rice pudding is a common dessert in Colombia. So are thin wafers called *obleas*. Desserts pair nicely with one of the most popular drinks in Colombia—coffee.

FACT!
Obleas are often served with a sweet sauce called arequipe, also called dulce de leche.

Shown here is an arepa served for breakfast.

GLOSSARY

civilization: An organized society.

climate: Long-term weather patterns in a place.

displacement: The act of removing people from their homes or homelands.

diversity: The quality or state of having many different types, forms, or ideas.

drought: A period of time during which there is very little or no rain.

economy: The way in which goods and services are made, sold, and used in a country or area.

export: To sell something from one country to another.

influence: To have an effect on the condition or development of something.

multigenerational: Involving more than one generation of a family, such as children, parents, and grandparents.

progressive: Using or interested in new and modern ideas.

rodent: A furry animal with large front teeth.

tradition: A way of thinking, behaving, or doing something that's been used by people in a particular society for a long time.

tropical: Warm and wet.

FIND OUT MORE

Books

Layton, Christine. *Travel to Colombia*. Minneapolis, MN: Lerner Publications, 2024.

Mather, Charis. *A Visit to Colombia*. Minneapolis, MN: Bearport Publishing, 2024.

Silva, Sadie. *Carnival*. New York, NY: Enslow Publishing, 2023.

Websites

Colombia
kids.nationalgeographic.com/geography/countries/article/colombia
Learn more fun facts about life in Colombia with *National Geographic Kids*.

Colombia Facts
www.kids-world-travel-guide.com/colombia-facts.html
Check out exciting information about Colombia, written by young kids like you!

Video

Capybaras in the Wetlands
www.pbs.org/video/capybaras-wetlands-shqkc8/
Check out the capybaras that live in Colombia's wetlands.

Publisher's note to educators and parents: Our editors have carefully reviewed these websites to ensure that they are suitable for students. Many websites change frequently, however, and we cannot guarantee that a site's future contents will continue to meet our high standards of quality and educational value. Be advised that students should be closely supervised whenever they access the internet.

INDEX